D1539312

Our Environment

Pesticides

Katherine Macfarlane

KIDHAVEN PRESS

An imprint of Thomson Gale, a part of The Thomson Corporation

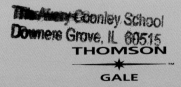

The Avery Coonley School
Downers Grove, IL 60515

THOMSON

™

GALE

Detroit • New York • San Francisco
New Haven, Conn. • Waterville, Maine • London

© 2007 Thomson Gale, a part of The Thomson Corporation.

Thomson and Star Logo are trademarks and Gale and KidHaven Press are registered trademarks used herein under license.

For more information, contact
KidHaven Press
27500 Drake Rd.
Farmington Hills, MI 48331-3535
Or you can visit our Internet site at www.gale.com

ALL RIGHTS RESERVED.
No part of this work covered by the copyright hereon may be reproduced or used in any form or by any means—graphic, electronic, or mechanical, including photocopying, recording, taping, Web distribution, or information storage retrieval systems—without the written permission of the publisher.

Every effort has been made to trace the owners of copyrighted material.

LIBRARY OF CONGRESS CATALOGING-IN-PUBLICATION DATA

Macfarlane, Katherine.
  Pesticides / by Katherine Macfarlane.
    p. cm.—(Our environment)
  Includes bibliographical references and index.
  ISBN 978-0-7377-3619-9
  1. Pesticides—Environmental aspects—Juvenile literature. 2. Pesticides—Juvenile literature. I. Title.
  QH545.P4.M27 2007
  577.27'9—dc22

2007006802

ISBN-10: 0-7377-3619-4

Printed in the United States of America

contents

chapter one

What Are Pesticides?

A **pest** is any plant or animal that causes damage to humans, crops, or domestic animals like cattle and sheep. Many pests are insects that eat grain, fruits, and vegetables. Insect **larvae** (caterpillars) also can be pests. Some insect pests, like the boll weevil, threaten crops grown for other purposes, like cotton used to make fabrics. Other insects, like cockroaches and ants, invade the places where we store food and spread dirt and disease. Some insects carry diseases to humans and animals. For example, some types of mosquito spread malaria, a disease that kills thousands of people in tropical countries every year.

Not all pests are insects. Some mammals, such as rats and mice, are pests. They destroy food supplies and spread disease. Weeds that use water, sun, and soil minerals needed by crops are also pests. So are weeds that are harmful to animals that eat them. Some types of fungus are pests, like mold and mildew.

A **pesticide** is any substance that kills a pest or keeps it from growing. Most pesticides in use today are chemicals that act as poisons to kill harmful plants, insects, or animals. Pesticides are sprayed onto fields to destroy weeds before farmers plant their crops or are used on crops to kill insects. They are also put into bait to poison cockroaches, rats, and mice.

(Right) Some mammals, such as rats and mice, destroy food supplies and spread disease. (Bottom) Some types of mosquito spread malaria, which causes over one million deaths worldwide every year.

The First Pesticides: Let Us Spray!

For thousands of years, people used natural methods to discourage pests. These methods did not wipe out pests, but they kept them from becoming a problem. The most effective of these methods fooled the pests by not letting them get enough food to breed in large numbers. Farmers planted their crops either early in the year, before pest insects hatched, or late in the year, after pests had completed their life cycle and died. They also planted several different kinds of crops in a field, so insects that ate only one kind of crop would have a harder time finding food. In addition, they mixed their crops with plants like chrysanthemums, which repel or kill pests.

One of the farmers' most effective methods for controlling pests was called **crop rotation**. With this method, the crops in a field were changed (or rotated) from year to year, so insects that ate a certain kind of plant would be unable to find food for several years and eventually died off. Thus, although farmers never completely got rid of the pests, crop rotation kept them from breeding in large numbers.

By the late 1800s, the human population had grown and many people were living in cities instead of on farms. To provide food for all these people, farmers began to use a new method of growing crops. Instead of planting several different crops on their land each year and using crop rotation, they planted fields with the same kind of crop and grew that crop year after year. This kind of farming is called **monoculture**.

Monoculture made pests very happy. They had plenty to eat, and sometimes their numbers increased rapidly. When that happened, they became a serious threat to the food supply.

Farmers looked for a way to control pests that thrived on monoculture. They began to use chemicals that could be sprayed or dusted onto the crops. These were the first pesticides. The farmers were pleased with how easily these pesticides wiped out pests.

There was only one problem with these early pesticides. They were made from compounds of **arsenic**, which is a heavy metal similar to lead. Like lead, arsenic is extremely poisonous. Although these arsenic-based pesticides killed the pests, they also left poisonous **residues** on food. Arsenic-based pesticides

Pesticides can move through the environment through soil, wind, and water.

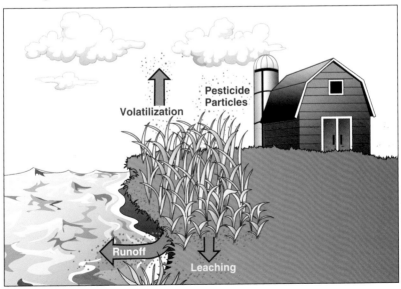

are hard to get rid of once they have been applied. They stay in the soil and are spread by the wind when it blows dust from the fields. They also seep into groundwater and well water. They get washed into streams and rivers, which carry them into the ocean. Today people are still having problems with arsenic residues left over from the 1800s. One example is when new houses are built on land that was once used for farming.

These early pesticides did not cause serious problems because they were not used all the time. Farmers used them only to control serious outbreaks, such as the potato beetle infestation of 1867. Still, people were not happy about spraying arsenic and other poisons on their food. They kept searching for a safer way of destroying pests. With the discovery of a pesticide called DDT, they thought they had found it.

The DDT Revolution

DDT was discovered by a Swiss chemist in 1939. He sent the chemical to the U.S. government, which first used it for disease control. American soldiers in World

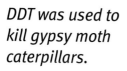

DDT was used to kill gypsy moth caterpillars.

War II were given cans of DDT to sprinkle on their clothes so they would not catch diseases carried by lice.

After the war, people began to find many more uses for DDT. It was dusted and sprayed on crops. It was sprayed on trees to kill gypsy moth caterpillars, which devour the leaves. It was sprayed on marshes to control mosquitoes. Housewives used DDT "bombs" to kill flies, which carried a deadly disease called polio that caused paralysis and death in children. DDT was called "the killer of killers" and "the atomic bomb of the insect world."

DDT was a very efficient **insecticide**, or pesticide that kills insects. Because DDT worked so well, and because it was cheap and easy to use, people used a lot of it. They even used DDT when it was not needed. Farmers sprayed the insecticide on fields whether there were pests there or not. They thought it was better to spray to prevent pests from appearing. DDT was sprayed on trees and bushes in neighborhoods where people lived, whether or not the people who lived there wanted it. It seemed like a good idea to use a lot of DDT because it was supposed to be safe.

New Pesticides

DDT was the first of many **chemical pesticides**. Chemical pesticides are made from petroleum (oil) combined with other chemicals, such as chlorine and phosphorus. Scientists developed chemical insecticides that were related to DDT, like chlordane, dieldrin, aldrin, parathion, and malathion. These insecticides work by poisoning the insect's nervous system. Some of these chemicals had first been discovered by German scientists researching nerve gas to use as a weapon during World War II. The new pesticides were many times more poisonous than DDT.

Scientists also developed new **herbicides**, or pesticides that kill weeds. Instead of using natural methods to kill weeds, farmers soon began spraying their fields with herbicides before planting. Spraying herbicides did not cost much, and it was a lot less work than plowing weeds under. Plowing also left furrows, which made it easier for rain to wash away the fertile topsoil and cause erosion.

Certain types of insecticides work by poisoning an insect's nervous system. They can prevent the nerves from signaling to the muscles that control the pest's breathing.

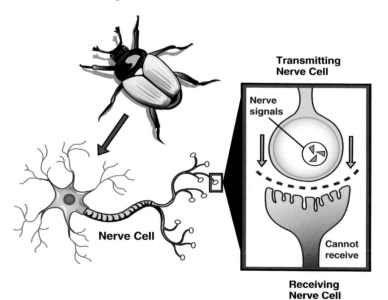

Transmitting Nerve Cell

Nerve signals

Nerve Cell

Cannot receive

Receiving Nerve Cell

Pesticide spraying in a greenhouse.

Too Much of a Good Thing?

In the years following World War II, American farms became more productive than ever before. The new pesticides were partly the reason for this. Farmers used a lot of pesticides to keep their farms producing well.

Companies found that making pesticides was a good way to make a lot of money. They started urging farmers to use more and more pesticides. Whenever farmers had problems with pests, they asked the pesticide salesmen what to do, and the salesmen told them that the answer was to use more pesticides and stronger pesticides. Hardly anybody thought that this could cause serious problems. But a few people started to notice some bad effects of pesticide use.

chapter two

The Dangers of Pesticide Use

Rachel Carson was a biologist and writer who worked for the U.S. Fish and Wildlife Service. In January 1958 she received a very disturbing letter from her friend Olga Huckins. Huckins owned a small bird refuge in Massachusetts. Earlier that year, planes spraying DDT to control gypsy moths had drenched her bird refuge with the pesticide. Soon afterward, Huckins and her husband noticed that songbirds in their sanctuary were dropping dead. As Huckins wrote in her letter, "All of these birds died horribly, and in the same way. Their bills gaping open and their splayed claws were drawn up to their breasts in agony."[1]

Huckins asked Carson if she knew any way to stop the spraying. To help her friend, Carson did some research to find out what DDT and the other

A plane dusts a field with pesticides.

chemical pesticides can do to birds and other wildlife.

Killing More than Pests

Rachel Carson discovered that pesticides had killed not only pests but also harmless and helpful animals, birds, and insects. Thousands of songbirds died in the early spraying of pesticides, as did squirrels, rabbits, and even house pets like cats and dogs. Pesticides killed beneficial insects like bees as well as ladybugs and mantises, which are natural enemies of pests. Fish died in the streams of forests that were sprayed with pesticides.

Sometimes creatures were poisoned indirectly through their food supply. For example, after a

Pesticides kill beneficial insects such as ladybugs, which are natural enemies of pests.

spraying of DDT to combat Dutch elm disease in 1954, dead robins were found all over the Michigan State University campus in East Lansing, Michigan. The insecticide had soaked into the ground and poisoned earthworms, which are a main source of food for robins. To make the situation more tragic, the robins that survived were unable to raise families. The poison caused them to lay eggs with shells so thin that they broke from the weight of the parents sitting on them. After a direct application of DDT to the bark of the elm trees in the autumn of 1957, birds like nuthatches, chickadees, and creepers, which eat insects in the bark, died because their food supply was poisoned by the DDT.

More deadly than the immediate damage caused by chemical pesticides is their **persistence**. Pesticides like DDT do not break down into harmless chemicals over time. Where they have been sprayed, these dangerous chemicals persist as residues in the soil and on plants, trees, and produce. Even many years later the land where pesticides were sprayed remains **toxic**

Bark beetle tunnels are revealed beneath the bark of a tree infected with Dutch elm disease.

)isonous). Pesticides are also washed into streams and rivers, where they can poison fish. The chemicals soak into the ground, where they get into the groundwater and contaminate springs and wells. Finally, they are carried into the ocean.

Poisoning the Food Chain

Rachel Carson also found that poisonous residues may remain on foods that are sprayed with pesticides. Many pesticides cannot be removed simply by washing the food. Some chemicals are absorbed into fruits and vegetables, so that cutting the peel off does not get rid of them.

Biologist Rachel Carson alerted people to the dangers of chemically treated agriculture, like these corn kernels treated with mercury oxide, a poison used as a pest deterrent before the 1960s.

*These Peregrine falcon eggshells were thinned due to
DDT exposure.*

Because their residues remain on fruits, vegetables, and grains, pesticides can get into the bodies
of animals that eat the produce, including humans.
The body cannot break down or get rid of the pesticides, so they are stored in fatty tissue. If an animal that eats pesticide is a food animal, the
poisons in its body are passed along to whatever
creature eats it, and the level of poison builds up.
For example, if fish eat insects or other organisms
that are contaminated with pesticide, they store
the poison in their bodies and pass it along to

whatever eats them, such as birds of prey. After DDT was sprayed on forests and streams that fed into rivers and the ocean, **ornithologists** (scientists who study birds) observed that fish-eating eagles along major rivers and coastal areas were having trouble raising chicks. Like the robins in Michigan, the pesticides caused these birds to lay eggs with shells too thin to hatch.

If cattle eat feed that has been sprayed with pesticides, the poison is absorbed into their fat and contaminates their milk. If the milk is made into butter, the level of poison increases because it is concentrated in butter fat, the fattiest part of the milk. When ocean fish eat plankton contaminated with pesticides and then in turn are eaten by bigger fish, the amount of poison is concentrated. These fish, like beef and butter, are eaten by people. Humans are at the top of the food chain and therefore absorb and store the most poisons of all animals in the chain.

Health Problems

When the government claimed that DDT and the other chemical pesticides were safe, the effects of pesticide exposure were not known. No research had been done. The research started by Rachel Carson and continued by other scientists showed that the effects of pesticide exposure can be deadly. As Carson noted, immediate exposure causes sickness and death in people who do not take care to protect themselves from the poisons they work with. For example, a gardener who regularly sprayed his yard with DDT and malathion developed permanent nerve damage and muscular weakness. Carson noted that DDT alone affects the central nervous system, resulting in muscle tremors or even convulsions as well as severe joint pain and mental symptoms such as anxiety and confusion.

Pesticide residues have been linked to a number of diseases that are caused by long-term exposure

These bananas are covered with a plastic sheet to protect workers from the chemicals that have been sprayed on the fruit.

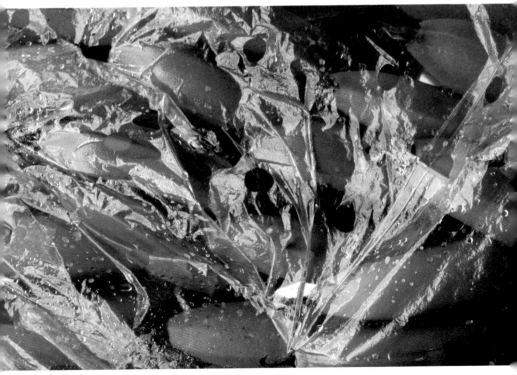

to toxic substances. Because pesticides damage the liver, they have been linked to **chronic** (long-term) liver failure. Pesticides that are sprayed in combination with other pesticides are particularly deadly. At the time of Rachel Carson's research, pesticides had been suspected of causing cancer. Today they have been linked to certain kinds of cancer, such as lymphoma in children and breast cancer in women. Pesticides also contribute to male **infertility**, or the inability of men to father children.

The more Carson learned, the more concerned she became about the poisonous effects of pesticides not only on birds and wildlife but also on people. Finally, in the summer of 1962, the *New Yorker* printed some of her findings in a series of articles. In September 1962 a complete version of her research was published in a book called *Silent Spring*. It was a wake-up call to the American people about the dangers of using DDT and other chemical pesticides. The book became a best seller.

chapter three

The Case Against Pesticides

Rachel Carson claimed that the best argument of all against pesticides is that they do not work over the long term. Only a few years after the use of DDT and other chemical pesticides became widespread, farmers began to notice that the pests had not gone away. If anything, there were more of them, and they did not seem to be killed by the concentrations of pesticide the farmers were using on them.

It turned out that some insects developed a resistance to the poison. Only those insects with a genetic resistance to pesticide poisoning survived and produced offspring, which also were resistant to pesticide poisoning. Carson wrote, "Under the stress of intensive chemical spraying the weaker members of the insect populations are being

Rachel Carson.

weeded out. Now in many areas and among many species only the strong and fit remain to defy our efforts to control them."[2]

Pesticide companies recommended dealing with the problem by heavier spraying of pesticides, stronger pesticides, and combinations of pesticides that were deadlier than single pesticides. These methods did not kill off the pests. Instead, they produced more types of pests that had greater resistance to more kinds of pesticides. Today a large number of pests resist one or more chemical pesticides. A few species resist all of them.

Rachel Carson was not in favor of eliminating pesticides completely. But she made a very strong case for banning chemical pesticides that were based on chlorine compounds, such as DDT, because they produced the most persistent pesticide residues. She was also very opposed to the overuse of pesticides where they were not needed.

The pesticide industry opposed Carson's book because it alerted people to both the dangers of its product and its inability to get rid of pests. By the end of 1962 alone, however, more than 40 bills had been introduced in different state legislatures to regulate the use of pesticides.

The Environmental Protection Agency

Inspired by *Silent Spring,* in 1962 President John F. Kennedy commissioned his scientific adviser, Jerome B. Wiesner, who chaired a group of scientists called the President's Science Advisory Committee (PSAC), to look into the pesticide problem. The PSAC's report in 1963, titled "The Use of Pesticides," generally backed Rachel Carson's findings. The PSAC supported the continued use of pesticides, stating that modern intensive farming methods required them. However, it also called for extensive study of pesticides and tightly regulated their use. It also recommended an end to the extensive, wholesale spraying that had been in use as well as the reduced use of those pesticides that persist in soil and water. It also called for phasing out the use of DDT and other chlorine-based pesticides.

Before the publication of *Silent Spring*, pesticide control had been handled by the U.S. Department of Agriculture (USDA). Because this department was favorable to the use of pesticides and worked closely with pesticide manufacturers, it did little to control the testing of pesticides or to limit their use.

As a result of the PSAC's findings, in 1970 President Richard M. Nixon called for the founding of a new board, the Environmental Protection Agency (EPA). Its mission was to establish and enforce environmental protection standards, promote environmental research, assist those fighting environmental pollution, and develop new policies for environmental protection. In 1972 Congress decided that the EPA, rather than the USDA, would manage the testing and regulating of pesticides. Later in 1972, the EPA banned the use of DDT in the United States. Later in the 1970s, the use of chlorine-based pesticides was also banned in the United States.

The ban on DDT and chlorine-based pesticides did not completely solve the pesticide problem. The EPA could not stop pesticide companies from selling DDT and other banned pesticides in countries outside the United States, such as Mexico, whose produce is sold in U.S. markets.

However, the EPA did see to it that pesticide manufacturers imposed much stricter tests on pesticides that were sold in the United States. It

An old can of household insecticide containing the pesticide DDT.

A scientist testing soil for pesticides.

also imposed its own system of testing on those pesticides that companies offered for sale. The solution is not perfect, but the EPA did get rid of DDT and the other chlorine-based pesticides, largely on the strength of Rachel Carson's arguments against them. The EPA is now moving to ban most phosphorus-based pesticides as well.

A number of environmental groups, including the World Wildlife Fund, Beyond Pesticides, and the Pesticide Action Network North America, are working to increase public awareness of the danger of irresponsible pesticide use. Their pressure on the government has resulted in several landmark acts to protect the public. Among these is the Food Quality Protection Act of 1996, which addressed the issue of guaranteeing safe food, especially for children. It stiffened regulation of pesticides used on fruits, vegetables, and grains based on the fact that children are more at risk than adults from pesticide residues.

Robins and other songbirds have made a comeback. Pesticides are not sprayed over people's homes and fields without their permission. Bald eagles, America's national bird, are no longer laying thin-shelled eggs, and neither is the California condor. Now that forests are no longer being sprayed intensively, the fish have returned to mountain streams and lakes. People no longer spray their kitchens with DDT, and those who must handle pesticides know to wear adequate protection. People have been made aware of the dangers of pesticide use, and more and more they are looking seriously at alternative ways of growing food that involve either fewer pesticides or no pesticides at all.

chapter Four

What Are the Alternatives?

Because of the problems that excessive use of chemical pesticides can cause, farmers and scientists are looking at other ways of controlling pests. They are using less pesticide, and they are using it more intelligently.

Less Is Better

The simplest way to avoid excessive pesticide use is to use less pesticide. Instead of applying large doses of preventive pesticides, farmers apply pesticide only when they actually see pests on the crops. They also use just enough pesticide to kill the pests, and they use local applications with tractors or hand sprayers instead of the earlier methods of large-scale spraying and dusting from airplanes.

Some pesticide companies are trying to develop chemical herbicides and insecticides that target only one type of pest. In theory, these pesticides are less harmful to the environment because they do not injure harmless plants or insects and are less damaging to birds and animals. They also need to be applied only where the target pest is found. However, these pesticides do not solve the problem of pest resistance. Pests can become resistant to these too.

Concerned about chemically treated food, many people are now buying organic produce.

Another way to limit pesticide use is to grow fewer plants that do not provide food or clothing but still require pesticides. For example, Americans spend billions of dollars every year to maintain their lawns. Lawns require regular applications of herbicides and insecticides to keep them healthy. In return, homeowners may get a beautiful carpet of grass, but the chemicals used to maintain the lawn can make the children and pets who play on it sick.

Alternative, chemical-free ways to landscape our homes include gardens with flowering plants suited to the local climate and **xeroculture** gardens, which use plants that do not need much water. Homes could also be built close to the street in front and finished in the back with a patio or deck, trees and flower beds, and a sanded play area with swings and a slide.

Organic farming has become popular because it avoids the use of chemical pesticides. Organic farmers are going back to some of the methods that people used to control pests before pesticides were developed. They also work with scientists to explore new types of natural pest control that attack pests without harming the environment.

Physical Methods of Pest Control

Another way to use fewer pesticides is to use **physical pest control** methods instead of chemi-

Plowing is a common form of physical pest control and requires no harmful chemicals.

cal methods. Physical methods of pest control are physical actions that either remove pests from crop fields or keep them from growing.

One of the most common methods of physical pest control is plowing, or tilling. Plowing fields before planting crops uproots and buries weeds. This method requires more labor than just spraying the fields with herbicide to kill the weeds. However, the spray-and-kill method requires the use of toxic herbicides and leaves weeds in the field, which then become homes for insect pests. Cleaning up the fields by plowing the weeds under gets rid of not only weeds but insect pests too.

Another physical method of weed control, used for low-lying fruit and vegetable crops like strawberries, is

Black polythene helps control weeds and insects in this strawberry field.

the application of **mulch** (a protective ground cover). When mulch is applied around crop plants, it retains moisture and discourages insects. An alternative is to cover the field with black plastic sheeting with holes through which crop seeds or seedlings are planted. The black plastic keeps light away from the soil so weeds cannot grow, and it also keeps moisture in. To debug crops like strawberries and tomatoes, some growers use a giant vacuum called the **Bug Vac** to suck insects off the plants.

Cultural Methods of Pest Control

Farmers who use **cultural pest control** methods manage pests by the way they **cultivate,** or plant, their fields. Many organic farmers are taking another look at older methods of planting their fields that are better than monoculture for controlling pests.

One cultural method that is coming back into use is crop rotation. Farmers plant different crops in their fields from one year to another. In this way, insect pests that feed on one particular crop are starved out when they cannot find food.

Another method is to grow more than one kind of crop in the same field. For example, a farmer may plant rows of a plant that repels or kills insects, like chrysanthemums, in between rows of crop plants. Farmers may also alternate rows of food crops with rows of **trap crops**. Trap crops are crops that pests prefer to the crop plants. The pests infest the trap crops and leave the crop plants

Farmers mix their crops with plants like chrysanthemums to repel or kill pests.

alone. Then, to kill the pests, only the trap crops are treated with pesticide.

Biological Methods of Pest Control

Organic farmers are especially fond of **biological pest control** methods, which use the natural enemies of insect pests instead of chemical pesticides to keep them under control. These enemies attack only insect pests and do no harm to other creatures. For example, farmers release **predator insects** into their fields. Ladybugs, big-eyed bugs, and pirate beetles feed on spider mites, aphids, and other small insects. Lacewing larvae are very good for aphid control. Small wasps destroy the eggs and larvae of moths, flies, and certain beetles.

Scientists are also experimenting with bacteria that cause sickness and death in insect pests. The most promising of these is *Bacillus thuringiensis* (Bt), which can be applied by spraying from an airplane. There are many types of Bt, each of which attacks one specific pest insect. Bt works very well. One program in Canada wiped out 100 percent of the harmful gypsy moths in the spray area.

Scientists also are finding out how to use insect mating habits against pests. To control pests like the medfly, males raised in a laboratory are either **sterilized** (made unable to produce young) or are **genetically altered** (have their genes changed) so that their genetic material will make their female offspring die. Then they are released in such large numbers that wild females are more likely to mate with them than with wild males. Females who mate with sterile or genetically altered males produce either no offspring or only male offspring.

Scientists also confuse male insects by baiting traps for them with **pheromones**. Pheromones are perfume-like scents that female insects give off to tell males of their species that they are ready to mate. The artificial pheromones in the trap are much stronger than those of the female insects. The males are drawn into the traps and die instead of mating with the females.

The Bacillus thuringiensis *bacterium has proven successful in controlling gypsy moth infestation.*

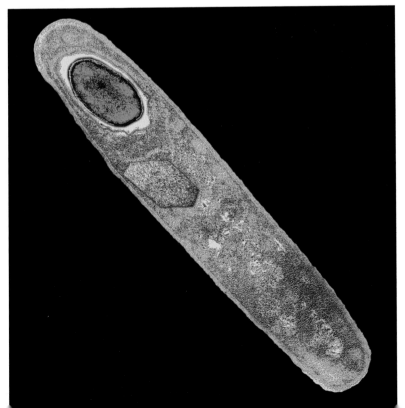

Genetic Methods of Pest Control

Genetic pest control is both one of the oldest and one of the newest methods of controlling pests. For centuries farmers have been looking for plants with built-in resistance to pests and selecting only those plants for seed. This is called **selective breeding**. It is an effective method of producing crops that are resistant to pests, but it is very slow. A faster method is to look for wild cousins of domestic crop plants that have built-in defenses against pests. These are then cross-pollinated (the plant version of mating) with domestic plants to produce a new plant with the advantages of both its parents. This is called **crossbreeding**. For example, researchers are crossbreeding domestic potatoes with a wild

Scientists can use genetic engineering to change the genetic makeup of a plant and create one that destroys specific pests.

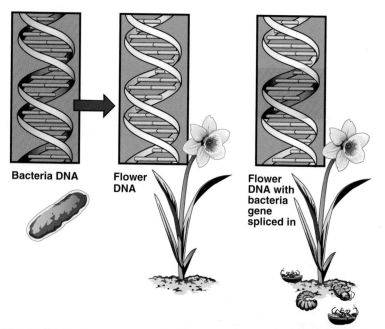

Bacteria DNA

Flower DNA

Flower DNA with bacteria gene spliced in

type called the hairy potato. The hairy potato is not edible, but it has such bristly stems that potato beetles and other pests cannot attack it. By crossing it with the domestic potato, the researchers hope to create a domestic hairy potato plant that produces edible potatoes.

A more advanced genetic method of pest control is **genetic engineering**. Scientists use this method to directly change the genetic makeup of a plant. For example, they have inserted genes from the Bt bacterium directly into crop plants. In doing so, scientists hope to make the plants poisonous to the pest insects that feed on them.

Integrated Pest Management: A Mixture of Methods

Integrated pest management (IPM) is a program that uses a mixture of chemical, physical, cultural, biological, and genetic pest controls. The idea behind IPM is that it is not necessary to kill every pest of every kind in order to produce healthy crops with large enough yields that the farmer can make a profit from them. It is only necessary to keep pests below a certain level.

IPM programs use low-cost natural pest control methods such as physical, cultural, and biological controls. They turn to chemical pesticides only in emergency situations.

IPM programs are set up by trained experts working with farmers and other people who will use them. Together they look at possible pest problems and figure out how much damage a given pest will do. They also look at environmental factors such as climate and soil.

IPM and other combination methods are more complicated to use, and they are more expensive than chemical pesticides. But over time they are much healthier for the environment because they do not poison plants, animals, humans, or the soil itself.

The Future of Pesticides

Scientists know that pesticides can be harmful to the environment. People and animals who eat foods that contain pesticide residues may become sick and even die. But chemical pesticides are likely to be the favored method of pest control at least for the near future. This is because large amounts of monoculture may be necessary to feed the growing population of the world. Chemical pesticides are necessary to support monoculture. As Rachel Carson pointed out, chemical pesticides are only a temporary solution because pests continue to build up resistance to them.

It is encouraging that farmers are beginning to use new, nonchemical methods of pest control. These new methods might increase as more farmers discover that they work and do not create the problems that are caused by chemical pesticides.

Notes

1. Quoted in Onlineethics.org, "Rachel Carson: A Scientist Alerts the Public to the Hazards of Pesticides." http://onlineethics.org/moral/carson/Huckins.html.
2. Rachel Carson, *Silent Spring*. Greenwich, CT: Fawcett World Library, 1966, p. 232.

Glossary

arsenic: A highly poisonous metal used in early pesticides.

Bacillus thuringiensis: A bacterium used as a biological pest control to kill insects.

biological pest control: A method of controlling pests by using their natural enemies.

Bug Vac: A vacuum cleaner that sucks insects off of plants.

chemical pesticide: An artificial pesticide made from chemicals.

chronic: Long term or lasting a long time; for example, chronic disease.

crop rotation: A cultural method of pest control in which different crops are grown in a field from year to year.

crossbreeding: Mating plants or animals with different but similar types to produce offspring that have desirable qualities of both parents.

cultivate: To plant crops.

cultural pest control: A method of controlling pests by how crops are planted.

genetically altered: Having the genes changed, usually by microsurgery.

genetic engineering: Directly changing the genetic make-up of plants or animals to produce desirable genetic traits.

genetic pest control: A method of controlling pests by changing the genetic makeup of plants or animals they attack.

herbicides: Pesticides used to kill plants; weed killer.

infertility: The inability to produce children.

insecticide: A pesticide used to kill insects.

integrated pest management: A program that uses a mixture of organic farming methods and chemical pesticides. It uses organic methods of pest control on a regular basis and resorts to chemical pesticides only in emergencies.

larvae: The immature, wingless forms of insects before they become adults; caterpillars. The singular form of this word is *larva*.

monoculture: A method of farming in which a single crop is grown in one or more fields year after year.

mulch: A protective ground cover made from organic material such as leaves or wood chips. Mulch discourages insects and weeds and holds in moisture.

organic farming: Farming that does not use chemical pesticides to control pests.

ornithologists: Scientists who study birds.

persistence: The tendency of a pesticide to remain on crops, in animal tissue, and on the land instead of breaking down into harmless substances.

pest: Any plant or animal that causes damage to humans, crops, or domestic animals.

pesticide: Any substance that kills a pest or keeps it from growing.

pheromones: Scents given off by female insects to tell males that they are ready to mate.

physical pest control: A method of controlling pests by physically removing them or preventing them from growing.

predator insects: Insects that hunt and kill insect pests.

residues: Substances remaining or left behind, like pesticides.

selective breeding: Allowing only plants or animals with desirable genetic traits to reproduce.

sterilized: Unable to produce young.

toxic: Poisonous.

trap crop: A plant that attracts insect pests away from crop plants.

xeroculture: Planting with dry-land plants that do not need much water.

For Further Exploration

Books
Rachel Carson, *Silent Spring*. Greenwich, CT: Fawcett, 1966.

Anne Witte Garland, *For Our Kids' Sake: How to Protect Your Child Against Pesticides in Food*. San Francisco: Sierra Club, 1989. Contains a comprehensive list of pesticides and their effects on the human body.

Lisa Yount, *Pesticides*. San Diego: Lucent, 1995. A well-written, balanced overview of the history, uses, problems, and alternatives of pesticides.

Periodical
Janet Raloff, "A Little Less Green?" *Science News*, February 4, 2006. Even so-called "ecological" pesticides cause damage.

Internet Sources
New York Times, "Rachel Carson Dies of Cancer; 'Silent Spring' Author Was 56," April 15, 1964. www.rachel carson.org/ index.cfm?fuseaction= obituary. An obituary of Rachel Carson that clearly describes the impact of *Silent Spring* on the founding of the EPA.

Onlineethics.org, "Rachel Carson." http://onlineethics. org/moral/carson/3-Action.html. A brief, clearly written account of the events that led Rachel Carson to write *Silent Spring*.

Public Broadcasting Corporation, "Fooling with Nature." www.pbs.org/wgbh/pages/frontline/shows/nature/disrupt/sspring.html. A concise overview of the impact of Rachel Carson and the President's Science Advisory Committee on the founding of the EPA.

Time, "Aroused Spring," May 24, 1963. www.time.com/time/magazine/printout/0,8816,830456,00.html. A good article on the findings of the PSAC in its report, "The Use of Pesticides."

U.S. Environmental Protection Agency, "Birth of the EPA." www.epa.gov/history/topics/epa/15c.htm. A concise and interesting account of the events leading up to the founding of the EPA.

Web Sites

Biological Control Information Center (http://cipm.ncsu.edu/ent/biocontrol). An excellent illustrated overview of biological pest control methods from North Carolina State University.

Pest Management at the Crossroads (www.pmac.net/humanimp.htm). This site's article "Pesticide Impacts on Human Health" provides a good general overview of the subject and is addressed to a general audience.

U.S. Environmental Protection Agency (www.epa.gov/pesticides). The EPA's article titled "Pesticides" provides a clear description of what pesticides are and the advantages and disadvantages of using them. It includes a list of pesticide types in use today and useful information on protecting children and pets from exposure to pesticides.

Index

Picture Credits

Cover: Photos.com
© Bettmann/Corbis, 22
© CDC/Phil/Corbis, 5 (bottom)
© Don Mason/Corbis, 13
Field Mark Publications. Reproduced by permission, 14
© Galen Rowell/Corbis, 17, 25
© Gary Braasch/Corbis, 19
© Hams Reinhardzefa/Corbis, 8
© Holger Winklerzefa/Corbis, 11
Illustration by Temah Nelson. © The Gale Group. Reproduced
    by permission, 7, 10, 36
© Najlah Feanny/Corbis, 29
© Patrick Johns/Corbis, 32, 33
© Richard Hamilton Smith/Corbis
© Roger Tidman/Corbis, 15
© Royalty-Free/Corbis, 26
© Staffan Widstrand/Corbis, 16
© Terry Whittaker; Frank Lane Picture Agency/Corbis, 5 (top)
© Visuals Unlimited/Corbis, 35

About the Author

Katherine Macfarlane holds a bachelor's degree from Stanford University, a master's from Columbia University, and a doctorate from the University of Washington. Nine years in the American Midwest turned her into a passionate environmentalist. She was very disturbed by the damage being done to the environment by the use of chemical pesticides. Macfarlane now lives in Santa Cruz, California, where most of the local farming is either organic or uses integrated pest management. Macfarlane enjoys watching birds on her seed and sugar feeders with her four above-average cats.